LIFE AT THE
TALKEETNA ROADHOUSE

By

Ronald C. Garrett

Talkeetna, Alaska

ALIEN PUBLISHING

Published by

ALIEN PUBLISHING

P.O. Box 10617

Spokane, WA 99209-0617

Copyright © 1998 by Ronald C. Garrett. All rights reserved.
Library of Congress Catalog Card Number 98-71197
ISBN 0-9770982-0-6

First Printing 1998
Second Printing 2005 (Revised)

CONTENTS

ACKNOWLEDGEMENTS AND CREDITS

ACKNOWLEDGMENTS AND CREDITS

These little glimpses of life at the Talkeetna Roadhouse have been a part of Talkeetna stories I have told to many people over the years. I had always felt a little sad that since most of the participants in these stories are dead, when I died these stories would be lost. One day when I was telling Roberta Sheldon, of Talkeetna, Alaska, of a little incident that happened at the Roadhouse over twenty years ago, she said I should write them down. I thought that was a good idea because once I had them on paper these stories would at least be recorded for future readers. I would like to thank Roberta for her suggestion.

I would also like to acknowledge and thank the following people for providing many of the photographs which are included: Trisha Costello, Jim Gleason, Jim and Suzy Kellard, Neal Menschel, Roberta Sheldon, Kathy Sullivan, John and Clara Wallace, and the Talkeetna Historical Society.

All of the photographs in this book were taken in the mid 1970s except for a few in the section, THE ROADHOUSE AS A SOCIAL CENTER. Some in that section are from the 1960s as noted.

VERNA & CARROLL CLOSE
Owners of the Talkeetna Roadhouse, 1975

INTRODUCTION

The Talkeetna Roadhouse is located in the village of Talkeetna, Alaska which is about 100 miles north of Anchorage along the Alaska Railroad. The village is located at the confluence of the Susitna, Chulitna, and Talkeetna rivers and has a rich history of exploration, gold mining, railroad construction, hunting, fishing, and mountain climbing. Gold was discovered in the early 1900s and Talkeetna became a supply center for the miners. In 1919, Talkeetna was connected by railroad to Anchorage. Also in that year the town site was surveyed and platted. In 1964, Talkeetna was connected to the Parks highway by the 14 mile Talkeetna Spur Road. Talkeetna was placed on the National Register of Historic Places in 1993. Located near Mt. McKinley, mountain climbers from all over the world come to Talkeetna in the spring and early summer to climb the mountain.

Verna Close came to Alaska from Washington State in 1936 and Carroll Close came from Oregon in 1941. They met and were married in Anchorage in 1946. They bought the Talkeetna Roadhouse in 1951 and operated it until they sold it in 1978. After the mountain climbing season of 1975, Carroll asked if I would like to work for him at the Roadhouse. He said he would give me room and board and pay me $3 per hour for the time I worked. I agreed and moved into room #1 in August. The population of Talkeetna in 1975 was about 250.

Some would say Carroll and Verna Close ran a tight ship at the Roadhouse. In fact, most would say they ran a very tight ship. Over the years they had developed quite a structured manner in their operation and they generally found little reason to deviate from their normal method of operation.

I wrote these short accounts of some humorous incidents I observed while at the Roadhouse so future readers might enjoy a little of the Roadhouse humor of those days.

After the sale of the Roadhouse, Verna and Carroll retired in Palmer, Alaska. Verna died in 1987, and Carroll in 1988. They were wonderful people and I hope you will get to know them a little better in these stories.

PEOPLE YOU WILL MEET   (ages in 1975)

Carroll Close 69   Owner/Operator of the Talkeetna
Roadhouse

Verna Close 66   Owner/Operator of the Talkeetna
Roadhouse

Ray Genet 44   Mountain guide from Switzerland. Came to Alaska and participated in the first winter ascent of Mt. McKinley in 1967. Founded and operated the first mountain climbing guiding service on Mt. McKinley. Died on Mt. Everest in 1979.

Jim Gleason 35   Local artist who moved to Talkeetna from California in 1972. Is quite well known for his excellent watercolor works depicting Talkeetna scenes, people, and life. Still living in Talkeetna.

Father Ryan 45   Catholic priest whose area included Talkeetna. From Ireland, trained in Rome and whose first assignment in America was Talkeetna.

8

Don Sheldon 53   Renowned glacier pilot. Moved to Alaska from Wyoming in 1938. Founded and operated Talkeetna Air Service for over 30 years. His biography, *Wager With The Wind*, was published in 1974. He passed away in 1975.

The author 34   Came to Alaska first in 1973 and returned in 1975. The reasons for this Birmingham, Alabama native being in Alaska are beyond the scope of this little sketch of Talkeetna life.

Talkeetna Roadhouse

MEALS AND SERVICE AT THE ROADHOUSE

Alaskan roadhouse meals are traditionally served family style at a long table. Everyone eats at one sitting and the food will be in bowls or plates that are passed around the table for self service. This tradition was strictly followed at the Talkeetna Roadhouse for the evening meal. Breakfast would normally be served in this manner with some exceptions for guests' schedules. Limited exceptions of course. Lunch was usually prepared for the guests or other customers at the counter and consisted of sandwiches and soup. People could order lunch at the counter and when they would ask what sandwiches were available, Verna would answer, "Ham, ham and egg, ham and cheese, and tuna. The tuna might be a little runny but it's O.K." Hamburgers were not served at the Roadhouse!

There were some restrictions on the food served at the Roadhouse. For example, no matter which way you ordered your eggs, they were always scrambled. That's just the way it was—no exceptions. Another was that the only breakfast meat served was very thinly sliced ham—no exceptions. Another, only vanilla ice cream was available. Once I asked Carroll why he didn't have chocolate and he answered that some people don't like chocolate but everyone could eat vanilla. A Roadhouse special was the Sunday night fried chicken. Incidents happening around this special event will be given later.

Another rule was that except for Roadhouse guests, everyone had to make reservations for dinner. Verna and Carroll would prepare the quantity for a meal for a certain number of people with reservations. If others came they would not be seated because there might not be enough food prepared. Some people couldn't understand why they wouldn't be seated when there might be several empty chairs. Most times, Carroll would lock the front door when the people were seated for dinner. The guests staying at the Roadhouse were told when dinner would be served and also told they should be there on time or they would be locked out and have to eat elsewhere.

Also, only Carroll and Verna would wash the dishes—absolutely no exceptions. Carroll always said if you gave a dish or piece of silverware to a guest and it was not spotlessly clean, they would never forget. They took pride in their Roadhouse and they assumed personal responsibility that the eating utensils were clean. When I first started working there they would not let anyone but themselves place the plates and silverware on the table. However, as time passed and Carroll gained slightly more confidence in me, he or Verna would lay out and inspect the plates and silverware and allow me to transport them from the counter to the table (about 10 feet) figuring I could not do too much damage in that short distance. However, he always walked around the table looking at everything as a final check before seating the people for dinner.

A special day, generally once a week, was when Carroll baked bread. To see him come in the kitchen wearing a white T-shirt and put on the white apron was the first announcement that it was baking day. Verna would ask how much he was going to make and he almost always said 21 loaves. I never understood the significance of 21 or if that was the number of bread pans they had but it seems as if every time he baked it was 21 loaves. Carroll did the entire operation while Verna would prepare the bread pans. Many times I watched as Carroll worked with the dough, Verna occasionally looking and perhaps making some comments, but Carroll always being in control. I wish I had a picture of him standing there almost completely covered with flour, his arms white, and a cigarette hanging out of his mouth. The aroma of the bread baking in the Roadhouse was wonderful. This was plain bread, very good and tasty, without any of the gimmicks or specialties of the present yuppie bakeries.

Carroll and Verna Close at the stove.

Roadhouse family style dinner.

Verna Close preparing breakfast.

Carroll Close serving dinner.

Roadhouse family style dinner.

15

WHERE TO PUT THE CHICKEN WINGS

The Roadhouse Sunday evening special was fried chicken. Carroll once heard a few local individuals say that they didn't eat anything all day so they would be very hungry Sunday night and could eat a lot of Roadhouse chicken. This infuriated Carroll because these same individuals did not eat at the Roadhouse many other times. They only waited until Sunday night and pigged out on the famous Roadhouse fried chicken.

I heard Carroll complain to Verna about these people and I finally noticed him taking action against them. He would not refuse to serve them but he had a clever way of combating their actions. Carroll and Verna always seated the people at the table for the family style dinners so Carroll would deliberately seat these individuals at the far end of the table. Then when he and Verna brought out the chicken, I noticed the serving bowls he placed at that end of the table were filled with mostly wings and backs. Most of the breasts and thighs were in bowls placed at the near end of the table, out of reach of the targeted individuals. I mentioned to Carroll that it appeared that most of the good pieces of chicken were placed at the near end of the table. He just smiled and said let them eat all the wings they want!

FATHER RYAN

Father Ryan was the Catholic priest who served the Talkeetna area and conducted Mass at the local church whenever they scheduled Mass. I always thought the Catholics adjusted their Mass schedule depending on the times of the National Football League games because my Catholic friends seemed to always see the big games on TV. Being a Southern Baptist from Alabama, I was taught to view the Catholics with suspicion. However, I made an effort to get along with the good father since Verna, being a Catholic, thought well of him.

I believe Father Ryan was from Ireland and had studied for the priesthood there and had later moved to Rome for study and was reported to be some type of Biblical scholar. His first assignment from Rome was to Alaska and Talkeetna. Father Ryan had been well trained in that he had an answer for any question or problem. When a question was put to him, he would pause as if trying to search his mind for the correct response he had been taught. I felt he knew the official Rome approved answer to any possible question that could be asked. I also believed that he truly believed these were the correct responses and I do not feel he would have ever deviated from the official church.position on anything. He appeared to be a good man who truly believed in his church and its teachings. His sense of humor had possibly been damaged or stifled by too much study and too much time in Rome but I feel his time in Talkeetna helped him to be a more understanding representative of his church.

At one local function where everyone was gathered outside on a beautiful day, I happened to be seated next to the good father. We were making small talk and he was telling me about Ireland and Rome when he asked about my religious background. I replied I was a Southern Baptist from Alabama. He stopped and thought for a few seconds and you could almost see the wheels turning in his mind to recall the facts, as taught to him, about the

Southern Baptists. After a few seconds, his eyes widened slightly and there appeared to be just the slightest hint of a look of fear in his eyes, and he said, "Oh!" We continued talking but I could tell his guard was up. I asked him, "How did you become a priest ? Was your father a priest?" He said " No," and then much louder, "No, of course not!" I did not show any response to his strong denial but acted like it was a fair question. He was a good man to talk with because even if you did not agree with everything he said or believed, you had to admire his dedication and conviction. Later, he did bring me a beer which I am sure would not have happened with my Southern Baptist preachers. As most readers will know, Southern Baptists think it is a sin to drink (taxed) liquor.

FATHER RYAN AND THE CHICKEN CAPER

Father Ryan was the Catholic priest for the area and as Verna was a Catholic, the good father had special privileges at the Roadhouse. For example he was given a salad bowl where everyone else had to use their plate for the salad. Another was that he was given hot tea where the rest had coffee or water. I'm not sure if Verna would have been considered a devout Catholic but she did attend Mass and the good father ate at the Roadhouse frequently, but particularly on Sunday nights.

Now Sunday night was special at the Roadhouse in that the evening meal (always served family style) featured the Close's famous fried chicken. When we set the table, Verna would always place a bowl and tea cup at the head of the table if Father Ryan was coming. I once mentioned to Carroll that it could be my imagination but it seemed to me that Father Ryan ate most of his meals there on Sunday night. He smiled and said he thought the Father loved the fried chicken. I mentioned that Verna always put the biggest and best breast pieces in a bowl just to the right of Father Ryan. He agreed and said he had noticed the same. I told Carroll I was going to do something tonight and to watch Father Ryan and me just at the end of his prayer.

When the table had been set and just before the people were seated, I asked Carroll to seat me just to the right of Father Ryan who would be seated at his normal place at the head of the table. Carroll asked why and I said just watch at the end of the prayer. I adjusted the serving bowl of chicken just to the right of Father Ryan to have the biggest chicken breast on top and the bowl was right between us as we were seated. I noticed him eyeing that gorgeous piece of chicken and could tell he wanted it. As usual, Carroll and Verna seated the people and then stood by the table. Father Ryan would always say, "May we say grace?" I always

21

had the greatest urge to say, "Not tonight, Father, let's skip it and get on with the eating." Of course I never said that but I wanted to. Anyway, the good father started on his prayer and when he started with the ending, I picked up my fork and stuck it in that large chicken breast on top of the pile. Father Ryan did his Catholic crosses at the end of the prayer and in a magnificently smooth, coordinated, and continuous motion, finished his crossing, picked up his fork and stuck it into the piece of chicken I had previously speared. He did this in such a fast motion that he did not have time to notice my fork was already in the piece and appeared very surprised to see another fork in the piece of chicken he was trying to obtain. As I had anticipated his action, I smiled at him and said, "Excuse me Father, I'll get this one out of your way." Carroll saw what I had done and it was the closest I had ever seen him to laughing loudly at the table. Rather than doing that and possibly having to explain his laughter to Verna, he put his hand to his mouth to stifle his laughter and walked out of the dining area through the kitchen and out of sight. Verna asked, "Where did Carroll go?" I said I thought he was getting something else. Carroll was gone a good five minutes before he returned to the table.

Talkeetna resident John Wallace with Father Ryan.

PROFANITY AT THE ROADHOUSE

Verna and Carroll Close did not use profanity, nor did they approve or condone the use of profanity by the Roadhouse guests or those eating there. There was a sign hanging from the ceiling over the right end of the counter that informed the public that profanity was not acceptable speech at the Talkeetna Roadhouse. I can remember but a very few occasions where someone used language that the owners felt was inappropriate. In those most rare incidents, Verna and Carroll tended to have slightly different approaches to addressing the problem. Carroll might simply approach the offending mouth and look at them and then point to the sign mentioned earlier. Verna, on the other hand, tended to take a more direct approach. She might hear words she did not wish to hear and she would immediately say something like, "Hey, we don't use language like that in here!" I don't know whether most people in there were repeat customers and knew profanity was not acceptable or just the atmosphere of the Roadhouse made profanity out of place.

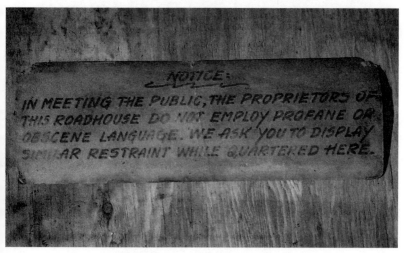

Roadhouse profanity sign

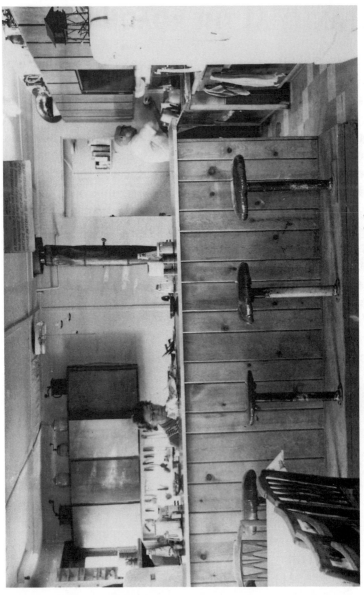

Carroll and Verna working behind the counter
The Roadhouse profanity sign is at the top

NORTHERN LIGHTS

One fall evening while I was walking around Talkeetna I noticed a glow in the sky. I went to an area away from any lights, and sure enough, it was the Northern Lights! I was very excited in that I had never seen the Northern Lights. As you will appreciate, they are rarely seen in Alabama, and I never saw them while I was living a few years in Washington state. I hurried back to the Roadhouse and rushed in to tell Verna and Carroll the Northern Lights were out, as we say in Alaska. Carroll asked if they were really bright and I said yes. (At least they were to me as this was my first view). Carroll slowly walked to the door and followed me outside and looked up at the sky. He looked for about five seconds and then he smiled and walked back into the Roadhouse. His smile sent me a message, "You brought me out here to look at this?" I guessed that after seeing the Northern Lights for over 25 years, perhaps he was not as impressed with this display as much as I was. However, he didn't laugh at me or make some caustic comment. He merely let me know quite politely that this was not one of the great Auroral displays of our time.

The following morning even the dog was not impressed by the author's account of the northern lights.

FRIDAY NIGHT AT THE MOVIES

Friday night was a very special night in Talkeetna because that was the night for the movie at St. Bernard's Catholic Church. The movies were selected and shown by Father Ryan. As the audience consisted of people of ages from about 2 to 92, the movies had to be appropriate for this audience as well as being appropriate for the place where they would be viewed. Therefore, they had to be reviewed and approved by the toughest censor of all, Father Ryan.

There was generally a big turnout since there was little else to do in Talkeetna on Friday nights. Families with all the kids would arrive and enter the church to get good seats. As in most gatherings of this type, the audience would divide into little groups and sit with their own group. The families with children would sit together in one area. Another area would consist of the teens, another of couples, and so on. The folding chairs were set up in a large room where Father Ryan and the projector were the center of attention. The projector was not at the back of the room facing a screen on an opposite wall, but more toward the center of the large room. Members of the audience would be around the good father as he showed the movie. Popcorn was available and it appeared almost everyone ate popcorn during the movie. The whole room seemed to smell of popcorn and burning candles. (Perhaps the smell of the candles was from years of services because I do not remember seeing any burning candles during the movies.)

As I said, Father Ryan selected the movies, so some of the adults were always interested if the movies might have any scenes which some (Father Ryan) might feel would not be in the best interest of the audience to view. On one very particular occasion, which I vividly remember, the movie had a scene where some young people were having a beach party at night. Some of them decided to go into the ocean so they started shedding their clothes and were running toward the water. The scene turned into one having about 10 or 20 youths running away from the camera and all we could see were a bunch of bare bottoms heading for the water. Father Ryan, who I was sitting close to at the time, made a little sound like a grunt or perhaps a slight gasp. Recovering, he quickly took his box of popcorn and placed in it front of the projector to block all of those bare bottoms. Of course, there was immediately a great howl from the audience at this blatant form of censorship. There was much laughter and someone even yelled, "Down in front!" The scene, and the blocking box of popcorn, only lasted a few seconds but to most adults, it was the best part of the movie!

RAY GENET AND PARKING

One morning, about 10 a.m. in the fall of 1975, I was driving my 1962 Dodge Travelall along Main Street in Talkeetna when I met Ray Genet driving his red Ford station wagon traveling in the opposite direction. We stopped in front of the Talkeetna Roadhouse to talk. I must add that for Genet to stop his station wagon was an event in itself. As the brakes on the vehicle were extremely marginal, when they worked at all, Genet had developed a procedure for assisting the brakes. He would slowly shift the transmission toward reverse which would cause the vehicle to come to somewhat of a smooth stop accompanied by the sound of grinding gears, with the loudness of the grinding dependent upon how much pressure he applied to the gearshift lever towards reverse. When we had stopped, we were opposite each other blocking both lanes of Main Street.

After we had spoken a few minutes, another vehicle came up behind us and the driver blew his horn. This was a surprising event because in those days there was little traffic on a weekday at that time of day, or really, at any time of day. We looked back to see who this impatient jerk was but neither of us recognized him. He blew his horn again for one of us to move although there was plenty of room for him to pull around us on either side. After the second blowing of the horn, Genet suggested we go into the Roadhouse for some coffee. I said O.K. so we got out of our vehicles, leaving them opposite each other in the middle of the street, and walked into the Roadhouse. The driver of the other vehicle appeared surprised at our action but finally drove around the vehicles and went on his way.

We had coffee in the Roadhouse and talked with Carroll and Verna Close and completely forgot about our vehicles that were still in the middle of the street. After about 30 minutes of conversation and a few cups of Roadhouse coffee, we were still sitting there enjoying ourselves when Carroll walked over to the

29

door and looked out at the street. He looked for a short time and returned to the counter and said, "Where did you guys learn to park?" We all had a good laugh at ourselves for forgetting the vehicles and wondering who the horn blower was. We finally decided he must have been from Anchorage since no Talkeetna citizen would have been concerned. Others came into the Roadhouse and each had their own special comment about our vehicles in the road.

Ray Genet and his vehicle at the Talkeetna airport.

CARROLL'S CHAIN SAW

One fall day Carroll announced we were going into the woods to get firewood. He had also asked Jim Gleason, a local artist, to help us. Carroll would cut the trees in manageable lengths so Jim and I could get them into the back of the truck. He would later cut them in short pieces for splitting. He, and only he, would operate his chain saw and Jim and I were only there to load the pieces into the truck. Carroll was a small wiry man and his chain saw was fairly large.

Jim came over to the Roadhouse and we all had breakfast and discussed the plan for getting the wood. Many cups of coffee later, we finally left in the truck. We arrived at the site and Jim and I discussed briefly whose land it was and if Carroll had a permit, if required, if it was public land. We did not mention our concerns to Carroll as it might be construed as questioning the expedition leader. Also, if he became upset with us he might cut the pieces in longer lengths and cause us a miserable day. Anyway, Carroll selected a downed tree and started up his chain saw to cut the tree in pieces for us to transport to the truck that was parked about forty feet away. He started on the tree and from the cutting results, I, being quite a novice about chain saws, wondered if Carroll had forgotten to install the chain. Much noise and smoke but I couldn't see any damage to the tree he was trying to cut. Carroll stopped the chain saw and told us it would have to be sharpened. Jim and I sat patiently in the truck.

After about twenty minutes of sharpening, Carroll announced he was now ready to cut this tree. He made the first cut quite successfully but at the end of the second cut the chain saw kept going beyond the cut tree and into the earth and seemed to throw dirt at least thirty feet because pieces of earth flew near Jim and me standing by the truck. The third cut went much slower and I learned from Jim that running a chain saw into the ground tends

31

to dull the cutting surfaces. The fourth cut seemed to take forever and I thought the tree would catch on fire from the heat of the chain before it was cut. Carroll announced more sharpening was necessary so Jim and I took our customary position back in the truck.

Twenty minutes later Carroll started cutting again. I, of limited experience in these matters, thought the cutting was still going very slowly and mentioned this to Jim who immediately cautioned me not to say anything because a woodsman's chain saw and cutting technique were a source of great pride. So I remained silent and after a couple of more cuts, Carroll announced this one was ready for loading and moved off to another downed tree. Jim and I carried the few pieces to the truck and I could not help noticing that it was almost noon and there were only six pieces in the truck. After we finished loading, we started walking over to where Carroll was working and were immediately showered with dirt and clumps of earth. Jim politely suggested to Carroll that the chain saw appeared to be hitting the ground after the cuts whereupon Carroll said that it was only moss from the underside of the tree. I started to mention that if that were the case, there were rocks in the moss because a small one came out of the air and hit my cap almost knocking it off my head. However, heeding Jim's warning, I remained silent but took out my safety glasses and put them on whenever Carroll started cutting. Jim and I took our positions back in the truck while Carroll sharpened again.

Jim and I had to take special precautions during lunch. Carroll made his own sandwich that consisted of one piece of ham between two pieces of bread. Verna, however, made the sandwiches for Jim and me and she put several slices of ham in them. We had to be very careful that Carroll did not see our sandwiches or he would complain to Verna that she was putting too much ham in them. The Roadhouse coffee we carried in the Thermos bottles was strong and full of coffee grounds. No matter how hard Jim tried to store the bottles to allow the grounds to settle to the bottom or to carefully pour the coffee, we always ended up with a large amount of coffee grounds in our cup. Carroll always said his method for making coffee had the grounds go to the bottom and you could pour the coffee off the top and have a grounds free cup. I did not want to dispute this but the facts appeared to prove otherwise.

One constant in our wood gathering venture was Carroll's habit in spotting "widow-makers." These are trees that have been blown over or broken but have not fallen to the ground but are hanging against and are supported by other trees. Jim and Carroll had many discussions about the technique to safely fall these trees. I, being a novice but not completely stupid, could see the danger in these large, hanging, heavy objects, and would have liked to avoid them completely and would have selected less threatening trees. Carroll would spot one and walk over to it and tell Jim how he was going to attack it. Jim would always tell Carroll that he should undercut it and Carroll would generally state that was normally correct but he thought in this particular case, he could get it done quicker without having to undercut. I found something inherently dangerous about the term undercut when viewing a large, heavy, hanging object. But, being the novice, I said nothing but moved quietly back, and using a practical knowledge of trigonometry, estimated the radius of danger around the tree, and tried to maintain a distance of at least twice that. Jim mentioned to me that if one did not undercut these, there was a good chance that the movement of the tree would pinch your saw thereby trapping it in the cut. As Carroll brought only one chain saw, on several occasions we had the opportunity to use a maul and wedges to free it when it became trapped. Carroll and Jim had several discussions about the cutting technique but I can not relate them all because a lot of the time I was not present, having been sent back to the truck to get the maul and wedges. I remember one "widow maker" in particular when Jim and Carroll had a lengthy discussion of the technique to be used, so lengthy he could have probably cut up another tree in the time of the discussion. Jim stepped back a few feet and Carroll started cutting. I watched from my safe distance well outside the danger zone. Once again the chain saw was trapped in the cut and I was asked to get the wedges and maul. As I was going back to the truck, I heard the breaking of limbs and turned to see the tree falling with the chain saw still stuck. Carroll stepped to the side and Jim stepped even faster to the side. The tree seemed to fall, hesitate, and then fall again, and each time the trunk seemed to jump around with Carroll and Jim also jumping around to keep away from it. No one was injured and luckily the tree fell with the chain saw on the top so even it wasn't injured. We freed it quickly with the wedges.

We returned the first day with about ten or twelve pieces. When Verna questioned the quantity, Carroll responded that we had done quite a bit of scouting and we would get much more the next day. I think we went out about three times, with some days skipped because of rain, to fill the truck. Each day was generally a repeat of the first day with Jim and Carroll discussing strategy and my trying to remain out of harm's way.

Carroll Close

Jim Gleason

One of Jim Gleason's paintings of Main Street, Talkeetna

CARROLL'S CAR FOR SALE

One day Carroll announced he was going to sell his car. I think it was something like a 1966 Dodge or Plymouth, four door sedan. There was some talk that Carroll had won it in a poker game a few years before but I'm not sure about the history of the car. I do not remember if he advertised it for sale in the paper or just put a notice on the Post Office bulletin board but several people came to see it.

One man from Palmer was really interested in the car and drove it and talked at length to Carroll about it. He tried to get Carroll to lower his price but Carroll wouldn't budge. Finally the man made a final offer and when Carroll refused it, the man left. The next day the man returned and told Carroll he still wanted the car and would pay him his asking price. Carroll responded that the car was no longer for sale. The man got a little upset at this and asked why it wasn't for sale. Carroll responded that he had changed his mind and would not sell the car. The man could not believe what he was hearing and finally

Carroll's car in front of the Roadhouse. (Norm Schebel with Jeff and Joe Kellard nearby.)

after much discussion offered Carroll $100 more than he was asking for the car the day before. Carroll still refused to sell him the car, saying he should have bought it yesterday when it was for sale. The man finally left and I must say he was quite upset.

Carroll sold the car to someone else a couple of weeks later, and I understood that it was for his original asking price, which one might have to say, was very firm!

CRIBBAGE

Carroll and Verna Close played cribbage. Often at mid-morning or mid-afternoon when things might be a little slow, Verna would take out the cribbage board for a little diversion. It seemed they were always continuing a game, although I do not ever remember them ending a game, and I'm not really sure how a game is ended. I could not play and did not understand the game of cribbage but from observations it appeared that after dealing and looking at their cards they would reject a few and then start playing the rest. After each person played a card they would announce a number (it appeared to me that Verna seemed to always announce the last number), then move their respective pegs some number of spaces along the board. After this, it appeared the next action was to question each other on how many spaces they had moved their pegs. A brief review of the cards, number announcements, and previous peg positions would result in each of them projecting a sometimes not so subtle image that the other player had made a mistake. That group of cards would be turned over and the process would start again.

I witnessed the playing of many partial games, or whatever a 15 minute bout of cribbage is called, and it appeared to my cribbage knowledge challenged mind that Verna's peg was consistently more advanced along the board than was Carroll's. I once was watching the action when evidently Verna had performed some spectacular feat and had moved her peg a substantial distance along the board and was projecting a very superior smile. Carroll was muttering something about having never seen anything like that in his life. I, attempting to add some humor to the situation, after Verna had moved her piece, asked, "Carroll, where is your peg?" Verna laughed and said, "His is way down there," pointing to a solitary peg some distance from where hers was located. Carroll looked up and said, without too much of a smile, "Don't you have some wood to split?" I suggested to Verna that if Carroll would use a larger or a brightly colored peg, it would be easier to find on those rare occasions when it was necessary to move his peg. Verna thought that was a good idea and told Carroll she would change his peg but she was afraid it might be stuck in the board since it had not been moved in such a long time. Verna laughed at her joke but Carroll, evidently not enjoying the humor, suggested that the game was not over and that they would continue it later and would see who had the last laugh.

Verna and Carroll Close

SPLITTING WOOD

One day in late September 1975, while I was gainfully employed for Carroll Close at the Talkeetna Roadhouse, Carroll told me he wanted me to split some wood for the Roadhouse wood stoves. We went outside to look at the wood and where the split wood was to be stacked. The wood was in the round and had been cut in about 18" lengths and was somewhat dry. Carroll, showing some doubt about my wood splitting experience or expertise, proceeded to instruct me on the learned techniques he had developed over many years of wood splitting. He selected a wide short piece to function as a base and then placed a piece on it to be split, stabilized it with his foot, and then with a well aimed blow of the ax, cleanly split the piece. He then picked up one of the split pieces, replaced in on the base, again stabilized it with his foot, and split it. He repeated this with the other initially split piece so that he now had four pieces. He told me that was the way experts split wood. However, he continued, since he could see that I was not an expert, I should not stabilize the pieces with my foot as I might cut off my foot with one of my wild swings of the ax.

Carroll went back into the Roadhouse and left me with what looked like the Mt. Everest of wood piles. I used the base piece he had selected and started splitting the wood. After about 30 minutes, being a fast learner, I realized that the constant bending over to pick up each split piece was going to do a number on my back. I took a break and contemplated my situation. I did not want to complain to Carroll that if I continued I might be worthless for a few days because I would probably have a very sore back. Since Carroll was about 35 years older than I, he would probably have been less than sympathetic. Then I suddenly had a brilliant (to me) thought. Along the wood pile was a long log that had not been cut. I thought I would stack 20 or 30 rounds to be split on the ground against this log and using it as a brace, perhaps the pieces being split would not fall over and I could

41

split them the second time without having to bend over and reposition them. At the least, I would not have to pick up each piece to reposition it on the base. It worked like a charm! I was setting up the pieces and going along splitting them like a machine on an assembly line. After each set had been split, I would get down on my knees and pitch them into the storage area without having to bend over. (Carroll said I was not to stack the split wood because he knew best how to stack it for the right combination of drying, appearance, and stability. I think his main concern was stability but he was just being kind not to suggest that he didn't think I could stack the wood without it later falling over.)

I continued with my assembly line wood splitting technique when Verna came outside. She asked what I was doing and after I explained, she said she thought that was a good idea. Carroll came out at that time and Verna told him how impressed she was with the way I was splitting the wood and perhaps he should try it this way because he always complained about a sore back after he split wood. Carroll looked quite annoyed at the scene and Verna's suggestion and said, "That's no way to split wood," and walked back into the Roadhouse. Verna just laughed and said, "Split it any way you want to, at least Carroll won't be complaining about a sore back."

Carroll Close giving instructions to the author on splitting wood.

GET THE BIRCH

One day Carroll was cooking on the wood stove and as I walked by he said, "Go out to the woodpile and bring me a couple of pieces of that split birch." I walked outside and looked at the large pile of split wood. Now I knew there were three types of wood in the pile: birch, spruce, and a small amount of cottonwood. As I have said, I am not a wood expert so I was experiencing some concern over my ability to differentiate these woods. I did not want to face Carroll with the wrong wood but I had to take something back inside to him. I searched my brain for any clues that I could use in the selection. Let's see, cottonwood, most people don't think much of it and say it always looks rotten. Birch, the Indians make birch bark canoes, white bark, now I'm on track. The only problem was these pieces were barkless, perhaps being old and dry, all of the bark had fallen off. Spruce, let's see, doesn't look rotten and no white bark. Not a lot of help there! Every piece I looked at seemed without bark but a few did look a little rotten. O.K., I had to do something because I didn't want Carroll to come outside and find me looking at the woodpile.

My mind was divided between taking two pieces of the same type of non-rotten looking wood and having a 50-50 chance of being correct or taking one piece each of the two types of non-rotten wood and hoping Carroll would accept that I picked up the incorrect piece by mistake. I chose the second option because at least it was somewhat defensible. I selected two different pieces and walked back inside to give them to Carroll. He took a glance at what I had and said, "I said two pieces of birch, you've got a piece of spruce. Give me the birch and take the spruce back and bring another piece of birch." Panic city! I knew I probably had a piece of each but which was which? My mind was racing for a response that would not show that I did not know the difference. Finally a solution, I appeared to stumble and I dropped both pieces on the floor at Carroll's feet. He asked if I was O.K. and bent over and picked up one piece and put it into the wood stove. I quickly picked up the other piece and left, telling him I would be right back. I approached the wood pile with confidence, feeling that through brilliant thought, I had avoided an embarrassing situation.

Now all I had to do was find a non-rotten looking piece of wood that did not look like the piece I was holding. I started looking through the pile and, oh my God, it appeared the piece I was holding had been cloned because every piece in the wood pile looked like this one. I realized that was impossible but I could not locate another piece that I could with complete confidence take back to Carroll. I agonized over this for a short time when I heard Carroll at the door say, "What are you doing?" I weakly responded that I was looking for a piece of the appropriate size like the one I had given him. He said the size wasn't that important and to just hand him a piece. The game was up! I had no action but to boldly walk over to the pile, pick up a piece and walk back to the door and give it to Carroll. I knew that a blind person had a 50-50 chance but I also knew a blind person had a fairly good excuse to explain the mistake. I had none! I handed the piece to Carroll who looked at it and said nothing for a couple of seconds. Those seconds seemed like an eternity to me! He finally said thank you and walked back inside. I walked back over to the woodpile and sat down, wondering how such a simple task had caused so much stress in my life. I spent the next ten minutes looking at various pieces of wood, and I swear I could almost hear them laughing.

WOOD STOVE SMOKE

An early morning ritual was the firing up of the wood cook stove in the kitchen. It seemed Carroll did this most of the time but Verna did do it occasionally. On this particular morning apparently they both worked at starting the fire and then each of them thought the other was going to watch and tend the fire. For whatever reason, and regardless of who was at fault, an enormous amount of smoke was generated and filled the Roadhouse. I was the only other person there that morning so there were no guests to be bothered by the smoke.

I was walking down the hall toward the kitchen and dining area when I noticed a great quantity of smoke ahead of me. I quickly went through the side room where the TV was and entered the dining area where there was so much smoke that I could barely see Verna and Carroll over at the wood stove in the kitchen. I went back to the side room and picked up a fire extinguisher and rushed to Verna and Carroll's aid. I arrived at the wood stove and said, "Carroll, here's a fire extinguisher, is it a stack fire?" Carroll said, "No, there's not a fire, Verna let the wood stove get away." Verna immediately responded, "Carroll, you were watching the fire, not me." Carroll then said, "I helped you start the fire but I thought at least you could watch it." Verna said, "Carroll, you never asked me to watch the fire, you were tending it when I went to the back." Carroll muttered something about having to do everything and he wished everyone would work as hard as he did. There were a few other exchanges but as the smoke started to clear the mood lightened a little, especially after I went to open the front door and stumbled over one of the chairs at the table.

After a few minutes with the windows and doors open the smoke was down to a moderate haze. At that time Ray Genet walked in and said, "Carroll, you're baking bread today!" Carroll responded that the smoke was due to Verna's inattention to the wood stove but he had control of the situation. Verna immediately responded that in fact it was Carroll's fire and therefore, Carroll's smoke. Ray smiled at this exchange and said, "I wanted something to eat but my eyes are watering so much that I think I'll step outside for a few minutes." I went outside with him and we had quite a laugh. Another person went inside and we put him up to asking Verna if she was making her bread pudding. The exchanges between Verna and Carroll were repeated. Word of the smoke at the Roadhouse quickly got around town and some people would come in later and act surprised because they had heard the Roadhouse burned down. Everyone had a good laugh but Verna and Carroll. That evening after dinner, Ray suggested that since there was still some disagreement over who caused the smoke that morning, perhaps they should let me start the fire the next morning. For the first time that day, Verna and Carroll were in complete agreement that I was not to be trusted to start the fire. Ray gave me a big smile showing that he knew what the response to that suggestion would be.

MOUNTAIN CLIMBERS AT THE ROADHOUSE

Talkeetna is the starting point for most climbs of Mt. McKinley. Climbers are flown to the glacier base camp by one of several companies in Talkeetna which specialize in these glacier landings. Often in the spring and early summer several mountain climbers would be at the Roadhouse either waiting to be flown to the mountain or just having returned.

I am not sure exactly how Carroll Close felt about the mountain climbers. I know he liked their business but it seemed he often commented about how much they ate. He might make a comment to Verna after a meal if she saw how much a certain climber had eaten and Verna might reply that he needed to eat a lot because McKinley was a cold and hard climb. Carroll might reply that the climber had already climbed the mountain and Verna might reply that he was probably still hungry from eating all of that freeze dried food for two or three weeks. I observed many of these mini discussions on mountain climbers but it seemed this was just something that was occasionally discussed without any firm conclusions reached. Sometimes after Carroll had made a comment Verna would remind him that Ray Genet was a local climber and guide who ate there but Carroll never commented about him. Carroll would just say, "Well, Ray is different."

Once Carroll told me there was a "German" at the Roadhouse asking questions about Mt. McKinley and would I talk to him. I went over and answered some of his questions about routes and weather and told him I had a map of the mountain if he would like to look at it. He said he would so I left to get the map. When I returned I put the map down on the table and held out my hand to shake hands and introduced myself. I said "My name is Ron Garrett." The man replied, "My name is Reinhold Messner." Reinhold Messner, to those not knowledgeable about mountain climbing, was probably the most famous mountain climber in the world. I felt a little foolish at not recognizing him but I had only seen pictures of him in books. Anyway, I justified, with all of the expedition mountaineering clothing and gear on, all climbers look about the same.

He and his climbing partner later left to climb the mountain and his wife (or girl friend) stayed at the Roadhouse while they were gone. She was a most attractive brunette who evidently helped Verna quite a bit during her stay. I remember Verna commenting about that mountain climber's wife was the hardest working person she had ever seen. She was always wanting something to do and appeared to have a great desire to stay busy. I included a photograph of Reinhold Messner in a group shot outside of the Roadhouse after their return from the mountain. Once the word got around Talkeetna that Reinhold Messner was in town, many local climbers came over to the Roadhouse to see him. They, like me, from the incredible climbs he had done, probably thought he would be some ape-like creature with his arms dragging along the ground as he walked.

Three famous mountain climbers and the author: Oswald Olz, the author, Ray Genet, Reinhold Messner.

The author with another famous climber, Mike Covington.

FLYING TO THE MOUNTAIN WITH DON SHELDON

During one of the Mt. McKinley climbs we were preparing to fly to the base camp with the legendary bush pilot, Don Sheldon. Ray Genet had me take the next three climbers to be flown in over to Don Sheldon's hanger. I had to drive Ray's Ford station wagon, which, as described elsewhere in this book, was an adventure in itself. The brakes, and I give them credibility by actually referring to them as brakes, were very inadequate to say the least. Luckily the terrain I had to travel over was completely flat so I had some chance of stopping the vehicle somewhere near my intended destination. (I later suggested to Ray that the vehicle needed a hole in the floorboard at the driver's feet. When he asked why, I said so the driver could stick a foot through it and drag it on the ground to stop the car. Ray did not think much of the suggestion but did admit he was going to have Gene at the Union 76 service station check out the brakes.)

When I safely arrived at the hanger, Don was fueling the plane for the next trip, and as always, he was straining the fuel through the chamois. He had fabricated a bucket with a chamois cloth on the top to filter the fuel. On the side of the bucket, near the bottom, he had installed a fitting to allow the filtered fuel to drain into the wing fuel tank. Don Sheldon carried this bucket everywhere he flew to make sure the fuel he was putting into his plane was not contaminated with water. This bucket is on display in the Don Sheldon exhibit at the Talkeetna Historical Society museum.

As the four of us approached, Don said he could only take three and asked which of us would remain. I told him I was the fourth and I would be on his next flight. We all helped load the plane and when it became time for the climbers to get in, Don

51

said the two shorter climbers would be in the back of the plane and the tallest in the front. Now you must appreciate how packed the back of the plane was with two people surrounded and wedged in with food bags, tents, personal gear and the like. The person in the front was quite comfortable sitting in the seat next to Don and having a great view during the flight. As they were leaving Don told me to have three more climbers there in about two hours for the next flight.

I returned and reported to Ray and told him the instructions Don had given me. Ray was busy checking some of the climbers' gear so he told me to pick two climbers to join me on the next flight. I looked over the group and selected the two shortest. At the appointed time, the three of us met Don at the hanger and went through the loading procedure. He looked at us and said, "OK, you two (to the short ones) get in the back." We packed them in and then I got in the front next to Don. As we were taxiing out Don looked over with a smile and said, "You didn't miss out on the tallest sits in the front, did you?" I laughed and said I did remember that. We had a wonderful flight to base camp and I did try to make the flight more enjoyable for my shorter companions in the back by describing the views they could only partially see from their cramped and packed position in coach.

Don Sheldon with the chamois bucket

Loading Don Sheldon's Cessna

Don Sheldon and Ray Genet playfully jousting after returning from the mountain
Photo by Roberta Sheldon

54

RAY GENET AND THE TENT POLE

On one of the Mt. McKinley climbs, the group was camped at the 14,000 foot level and in the middle of quite a storm. Ray Genet did not like to cook in a tent because of the problem of the stove using the oxygen and producing other gases not in the best interest of the climber's health. He always said if you cooked in the tent you tended to get a little stupid and might make a judgment error with serious consequences. Anyway, this storm had a lot of strong wind and with that and the blowing snow, cooking outside was practically impossible no matter how extensive a windbreak was constructed. So Ray gave up and said he would cook inside the tent.

I remained outside to hand in the snow to be melted for water and also to give him more room as he had three stoves going in preparing the meal for all of the climbers. This continued without incident for a short time but the storm seemed to intensify with stronger gusts of wind. I had on all of my heavy mountaineering clothing and wind gear so I was not unduly uncomfortable outside. I did have some thoughts as to why I was standing outside in a storm when everyone else was in the tents and obviously more comfortable than I. However, I did realize as the assistant leader, my position was to assist the leader, so I did as told and just tried to face away from the wind.

The tents of this period were the center pole pyramid type (REI McKinley tents) in that the main support was a single tent pole set on the floor and the top of the pole fit into a sleeve at the apex of the tent. The sides and walls of the tent were held up and out by nylon guy cords attached to snow blocks or gear around the perimeter of the tent. The tent bottom was attached to the ground (snow) by pegs driven into the snow. When strong gusts of wind would hit the tent, it would tend to rise and almost bounce. After one particularly strong gust of wind, I heard very strong language coming from the tent. I quickly turned around and saw that the tent, instead of being the normal height of about 5 feet, was now only about 2 feet high. The tent pole was sticking through the side of the tent. Ray was yelling, "Garrett, get this (x?!+*#) tent off of me." He was trying to keep the tent fabric off the stoves so the whole tent would not be destroyed. I quickly grabbed an ice ax and deftly stuck the end of it through the top center loop and immediately pulled it up and moved the tent off Ray and the stoves. While I was holding the tent up, there was some fumbling around inside the tent and additional words were heard which will not be repeated here. Soon, the center pole was removed from the side/hole in the tent and returned to its proper position.

After the situation seemed to have been stabilized, I went to the tent opening and looked inside. Ray was kneeling over the stoves trying to return things to their proper positions but he was still a little upset. "I spilled the hot Tang," was his comment. This was met with a wry smile from me (which I was careful to hide) because I was not particularly fond of hot Tang. Ray, however, firmly believed it was good for you and insisted on serving it each day. I went away from the tent and visited another tent and reported on the tent pole and the loss of the hot Tang for dinner. This was meet with a rousing cheer from these climbers as evidently I was not the only one getting a little tired of the daily serving of hot Tang. As a side note, on one expedition Genet severely reprimanded some of the climbers for peeing near the tents instead of using the latrine we had dug in the snow. He continued in that he would be watching for anyone not using the latrine. Later, in private, I mentioned to Ray that perhaps he might lighten up a little on the peeing situation. When he asked why, I replied that I did not think those were pee puddles but discarded portions of hot Tang. He could not believe that and/or would not accept that his climbers were discarding the hot Tang. I let the matter pass without additional comment.

Another interesting point was the repair of the hole in the tent. We had some rip stop nylon repair tape, which had to be applied with heat. I did not want to envision heating the repair tape with the stove flame and trying to apply the heated tape over the hole. Even worse was the thought of having the stove flame close to the hole in the tent (fabric). Being quite attuned to Alaskan methods of temporary repairs, I suggested we try to apply duct tape over the hole by sandwiching the hole from inside and outside. Ray did not think much of that idea but as usual, he was open to try anything. We got the duct tape from our repair kit and applied it as discussed. Not only did it repair (cover) the hole, the repair lasted the rest of the climb! We could always spot Ray's tent from the duct tape and it became known as the duct tape tent!

Camp at 14, 000 feet before the storm

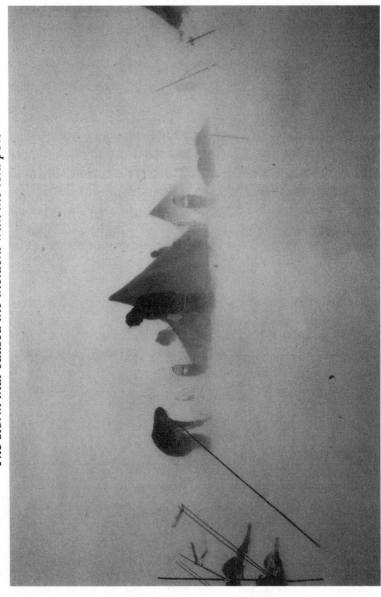

The storm that caused the incident with the tent pole

THE MISSING BRANDY

One fall morning after Ray Genet had finished breakfast at the Roadhouse, he was sitting at the table with Carroll and me. He announced that he had been checking the gear from the last Mt. McKinley climbing expedition and had discovered something was missing. When Carroll asked what was missing, Ray continued that in two of the summer expeditions, the medicinal brandy had not been returned with the community gear (Ray always included brandy in the medical kit). His manner appeared serious but Carroll and I both knew this was a ruse. Carroll said he did not think Ray allowed drinking on his mountain climbs. Ray responded that the brandy was a part of the medical kit and was only to be used for medicinal purposes and was not for drinking. I remained conspicuously silent because I had some knowledge of why the brandy was missing. Ray said that additional research showed that the two instances of the missing brandy occurred on expeditions of which I had been a leader. I asked if he suspected the staff. He replied that he suspected me!

Carroll, taking the bait, immediately replied that he was surprised that Ray would come into the Roadhouse and accuse his best worker of stealing liquor. Ray responded that I was his only worker. At that point, Verna, who was behind the counter, spoke up and said, "Don't I do any work here?" I quickly responded that Ray meant outside workers. She said "I hope you weren't meaning that my work didn't count." She appeared satisfied she had made her point and returned to what she was doing. The three of us took quick glances at each other knowing we had traveled on dangerous ground.

I asked Ray why I was the suspect when there were at least 14 other climbers who were in the groups. He said that one day when we reached the summit, after we returned to our 17,000 foot camp, I appeared too happy after dinner. I replied that I was happy that everyone reached the summit and returned safely to our high camp. He said again that I was too happy. At this point Carroll said that Ray had no real evidence against me and that he was ashamed of Ray for accusing me. Ray laughingly agreed and said he would join us for dinner that night at the Roadhouse. Carroll said Ray should buy me a drink later to make up for the outrageous charges. He said O.K. and when Carroll asked me what I would like, I replied, "Brandy, of course", after which we all had a good laugh.

Ray Genet welcoming the author back from a Mt. McKinley climb. (I think he already had a suspicion about the brandy.)

Ray Genet on the summit ridge, Mt. McKinley.

DON SHELDON'S MYSTERIOUS PACKAGE

During one of the Mt. McKinley climbs we had reached the summit and were resting the next day at our 17, 300 foot camp. Many of the climbers were in the tents but a few of us were sitting outside and admiring the view, as it was such a nice day. We heard a plane and finally saw Don Sheldon's silver Cessna flying nearby. We wondered what he was doing but remembered his reputation for checking up on his climbers. As he made a pass over the fairly flat area between us and the start of the slope up to Denali Pass, something came out of the plane and fell to the snowfield perhaps 100 yards away. Those outside who witnessed this wondered what he had thrown out or dropped. There was some discussion but as tired as we were no one wanted to trudge through the snow (at 17, 300 feet!) to find out. Finally as some of the climbers went into their tents, the climber next to me said he was going over to see what it was. I watched in admiration at his energy as he walked through the snow over to the mysterious object. I could see him standing over it and then he bent over as if to take a closer look. He then shuffled around a bit and started walking back over to us. When he arrived someone asked what it was and he said just an empty box. I immediately thought the object fell quite fast for an empty box but I said nothing.

Slowly the rest went back to their tents until only the climber who investigated the drop and I were alone. We were sitting and just chatting when he said, "Would you like some ice cream?" I said sure, and a steak and a cheeseburger if he had them. He said, "Really, do you want some ice cream?" A light began to go on and I asked (very quietly) was that ice cream he dropped? I remembered reports of Don Sheldon dropping ice cream to his climbers. He got up and told me to come into the tent with him whereupon he produced a half-gallon of vanilla ice cream. After

63

20 days of freeze dried food, Tang, and oatmeal, you can only imagine how appetizing that ice cream was. I asked if we should share it with the others and he said the others did not go over and get it so why should they get to eat any of it. I immediately recognized and approved his thought process. I did have some concern as to why I was so lucky as to participate in the eating but I quickly dismissed that thought and returned to the task at hand. As we ate the ice cream, we did discuss if we should save a small amount for the others but we both concluded there was so little left if we tried to divide it among the others it could cause some dissension. We therefore concluded in the interest of group harmony we should consume all of the ice cream and not disclose it to the others. After finishing the ice cream and licking the box like some animals at a salt lick, we then had to hide the evidence. He folded it and put it in with his personal gear

Later that day Ray Genet returned from a lower camp and asked the group if Don Sheldon had thrown anything out of the plane. There was some discussion and description of the search for the object and the bottom line was that the investigator said it was an empty box and I said nothing. Ray looked at me and I believe he was looking at my mouth. (Thank God the ice cream was vanilla as we used zinc oxide on our lips for protection from the sun) During dinner that night Ray commented that I did not have my normal appetite and I responded that my stomach was a little upset. He just smiled and said "Sure." The way he looked at me I believe he knew what Don had tossed out and that he knew that I knew that he knew. I do not believe the other members had any idea what had happened and it is probably a good thing because if they had, there could have been two more bodies left high on Mt. McKinley!

Don Sheldon

Ray Genet and Don Sheldon

WHY RAY GENET BECAME SO ANGRY WITH THE AUTHOR

The story began at 16,200 feet in the Argentine Andes. We (the climbing expedition) had just managed to get all 14 members of the team on the summit of Mt. Aconcagua (22, 920 feet), the highest peak in the western hemisphere. To get all 14 on top was an unheard of feat in those days, especially climbing via the Polish route, which is no walk-up! The party had returned and camped at this altitude and were planning to get an early start in the morning to hopefully travel most of the way back down to the Argentina-Chile highway where we would catch the bus back to Mendoza, Argentina. In addition to going down about 10,000 feet, the distance to be traveled was about 20 miles.

Members of the expedition

As we were resting around the tents, some members of another expedition came up from their 14,000 foot camp carrying equipment. They were Canadian, and after speaking to them, I learned that an old friend of mine, Chuck Petrie, was with their party and was in the lower camp. As Chuck and I had attempted Aconcagua a few years ago, and as he was such a great fellow, I was eager to see him again. I asked Ray if I could go down and stay at the Canadians camp that night and I would join back up with him and the rest when they came down in the morning. He said OK but asked that I take someone with me as he did not want anyone traveling alone. I took Don, a strong climber and friend from a Mt. McKinley expedition a couple of years before. We went down just behind the Canadians.

When I arrived at their camp it was good to see Chuck, especially when he opened a can of peaches. While canned peaches might not seem much of a treat, after 20 days of freeze-dried food(?), any fruit was a treat. Don and I stayed the night and had a good time talking to Chuck and the others and discussing the route and their plans. The next morning Don and I helped them get their gear packed and saw them off up the mountain towards the 16, 200 foot camp.

The author enjoying peaches, courtesy of Chuck

At this point things began to get a little confused. From thi camp you could not see the higher camp because of all of the humps and bumps on the rock and debris covered glacier. We went over to the trail, or what there was of a trail, but we coulc not see the high camp or anyone on the trail above or below Since Ray had planned on a very early start for this morning and since the Canadians had been a little late in their start, Dor and I were not sure if Ray and the rest had already passed us on the way down or if they were still above us. (Also I must adc you could not see the 14,000 foot camp from the trail). We waited a few minutes discussing whether Ray and the rest of the party were above or below us. We looked for tracks or any signs on the trail to give us that information but I must say our scouting skills were a little lacking. After some discussion, we decided to proceed down because we would feel a little stupic sitting there while the rest of the party was descending. (We later learned that because of the roughness of the terrain, the Canadians and the Genet party did not see each other because of some route variance along the trail). As we continued down, the topography was such that we could not see the entire route down because of intervening cliffs, dips, hills and other things As we continued on, I had a growing suspicion the rest of the party was behind rather than in front of us. However, we continued down always looking ahead or behind for the rest of the party.

After a few hours we came to the end of one valley and had to turn to the right and go down the large valley towards the road still some 12-15 miles away. We stopped and had a snack anc kept looking up and down for the party but saw nothing. As there was one slightly dangerous traverse along the river a few miles ahead, we decided to continue down to that area. We discussed the possibility of the others still being behind us but we rationalized that while it might appear that way, there was still a chance they were ahead of us. (In retrospect, some readers might think we were in denial, which I now might be more willing to accept as closer to the truth than I would have been at the time of the incident). Anyway, we continued on down the valley to the trouble spot. We passed it without difficulty and readily agreed it was not dangerous at all because the river was lower than when we had passed it going up almost 3 weeks ago. We continued on down and reached a small stone hut still about 5 miles from the road.

Because we were very tired, we decided to eat and sleep there overnight and wait for the others. We had some food, mostly freeze-dried, but were very tired of that. In the cache we had left near the hut when we first passed was some sugar and powdered milk. We decided to whip up a vanilla shake, so we added about equal parts of powdered milk and sugar and just enough water to make it drinkable. We drank entirely too much of this "shake" before going to sleep. We slept out in the open in our sleeping bags and I still remember the brightness of the stars on that incredibly clear night at about 8,000 feet.

I woke up with a start about 3 AM with my heart racing and was so hot I had gotten out of my bag. I could not figure out what was wrong with me and had some slight fear I was dying. Don moved a little and I asked if he was awake. He replied he was, but he was very hot and felt a little out of breath. I then had the thought we had been poisoned. We both got up and compared symptoms. After too long a period for normally intelligent people to realize the cause of the condition, we realized we were having a calorie or sugar rush from the incredible amount of milk and sugar we had consumed on a mostly empty stomach and slightly dehydrated body. After walking around a bit, we realized we were not going to get back to sleep, so we decided to pack up and start walking toward the road.

After a couple of miles we began to feel a little more normal and as the sun started to come up everything seem OK. As we dropped down lower in the valley we spotted a solitary Argentine on horseback. We stopped and spoke to him with some difficulty. I began to think he might be a little slow because we were having some problems in communicating. When I mentioned to Don that this fellow might be a little stupid, Don gently pointed out that it might not be his problem but ours, as this fellow had probably never listened to crude, broken Spanish spoken with an Alabama accent! I agreed he might have a valid point. Despite the communication difficulty, we did learn the bus to Mendoza (only one bus per day) was coming through their village at just about the time we would arrive there if we really hustled. We said good-bye and really picked up the pace to get to the military post where the bus stopped.

When we arrived at the post we saw the bus near the gate. We walked rapidly toward the gate and were met by a soldier pointing a rifle at us. We stopped and waited where we were per his instructions. There we were, standing in the dirt road about 25 yards from the gate and somewhat near the bus with all of the passengers and driver looking at us. I walked over to the bus and asked the driver when he was leaving for Mendoza. "Muy pronto," was the reply. I asked if he could wait for us, as we had to get our passports back from the military. In those days the military ran the country and if you wanted to climb Aconcagua, they held your passport until you returned. Finally the Commandante arrived at the gate and waved us up. We recognized each other as he had been there and taken our passports when we started the climb. I told him our names and asked for our passports. He asked where the other twelve were, acting as if he hoped we were not the only survivors. I assured him the others would be there soon and everyone was OK. He said he would hold the passports until everyone was there. I did not want to wait for that so I told him that my partner, Don, had some medical problem and that I needed to get him to Mendoza to see a doctor. I don't think Don understood what I was saying but I hoped it would be enough for the Commandante to let us go. He said that would be OK and he would go and get our passports. He was gone about 5 minutes and returned asking for our names as he had forgotten them. (I guess all Norteamericanos look the same) I wrote our names for him and at that time the bus driver started the bus and blew the horn. I rushed over and asked the driver to please wait, that we would be ready to go very shortly. He replied he had to leave immediately and we could get the next bus tomorrow. I rushed back to the Commandante and asked if he could please hurry in that the bus was about to leave. "No problema," was the reply. The driver blew the horn again and moved the bus a few feet. I again asked the Commandante to please hurry. Again he said, "No problema." He slowly walked over to the bus, stepped up to the driver and at that time the driver turned off the engine. The Commandante walked back over to us and smiled and said, "No problema." Fifteen minutes later he returned with our passports and walked over to the bus to see us off. The driver really glared at us and the other passengers did not seem very happy but when the Commandante walked up the steps on the bus and looked around, no one said anything. As I said, at the time, the military really ruled the country.

The ride to Mendoza was uneventful except I felt sorry for those unfortunate to have to sit near us because, as you remember, we had been on the mountain for about three weeks - with no bath! We arrived at the Mendoza bus station and took a cab to the hotel. After a great shower, some clean clothes, and a wonderful Argentine steak dinner, we were beginning to feel human again. As we sat drinking our wine, we discussed the others and were sure they would be on the bus tomorrow. Off to sleep- in a bed!

The next day I took a cab down to the bus station to meet the others but they did not arrive. I started to have some guilty feelings at that time so I had a little extra wine with my dinner that night to dull those feelings. I do not remember if Don left Mendoza for his flight back to the US the following day. However, I passed my time by the pool with some Argentine friends I had met when I was down for a climb a couple of years before.

To shorten the story, Ray and the others did not arrive until the third day. As it happened, they had arrived at the military post the day after us, but too late to catch the bus. They camped overnight there and were going to catch the bus the next day. Problem was, the next day the bus was full! I understand there was almost a mini revolt among the other members of the team when they realized they would have to stay at the post another night. I think Ray vented his frustration at Don and me (mostly at me as I was the assistant leader) while waiting at the post. I guess there was much grumbling about our enjoying the good life in Mendoza while they were still camping on a dirty windswept piece of earth near the military post. When a couple of the others did sort of reprimand me later for being in Mendoza ahead of them and having a good time while they were still in their tents, I responded that it really was not all that much fun and good times. After all, the wine with our steak dinner the second night was really not that good. This did not help soothe the feelings!

During the couple of days the group remaining was all together at the hotel, Ray did not speak to me except to say that I had deserted the expedition. His girlfriend, Kathy, said he said he had expressed the desire to kill me when he got to Mendoza. I think that was probably a slight exaggeration of his feelings - at least I hope that was an exaggeration! Since Kathy and I got along well, he did not like us talking so he told her not to talk to me. The others in the expedition seemed to not really care that much and they were happy to be down and had travel plans and other issues to deal with of more importance. The others gradually left to return to the US and I took a flight to the South of Argentina and toured there and in Chile for about ten days and then returned to the US.

I worked on the Trans Alaska pipeline in those days so I was in Talkeetna very little. I did not see Ray for many weeks after I returned but I did see Kathy - who was pregnant! This woman, who was probably as strong as anyone on the expedition, had climbed the mountain while pregnant, I suddenly felt very old and tired! Anyway, she told me Ray was still mad at me and still felt I had deserted the expedition. I tried to meet with him to try to set things right but my work schedule and his travels were such that we did not see each other until later that spring. I was at my little cabin one day when Ray came and knocked on the door. I said hello, but before I could start any conversation about the climb, he announced I would have to leave Talkeetna. He said it wasn't good for both of us to live in the same town and that I would have to leave. I really believe he was serious! I told him I was not going to leave and that we would just have to get along. He said he did not want to talk to me or see me and to stay away from him and Kathy. He then left.

A few days later there was a knock at my cabin door and it was Ray again. He had an angry look on his face. Before I opened the door many thoughts ran through my mind. I was concerned he was there to fight. Now I was physically larger but he was an incredibly strong man and I did not relish the thought of fighting him. However, he was at my cabin so I opened the door and said hello. He had one hand behind his back, which gave me some concern, but he spoke. He said we had to get along and that not getting along was too much negative energy. He said he thought I was wrong to leave the group but he would put it behind us. He then brought out his hand and in it was a bottle of blackberry brandy. Ray did not drink much but he did take some brandy occasionally. We shook hands and I admitted to him he was probably right and I apologized. We both relaxed a great deal and walked out in the little field next to my cabin and started on the brandy. As the bottle of brandy became lighter, our differences seemed to dissipate. We spoke of some of the Mt. McKinley climbs we did and I mentioned the photo I had of him on the Kahiltna glacier - wearing a baby bonnet! He could not remember how he got the bonnet or who gave it to him. I laughed and said i didn't matter- it was the picture that mattered. He asked me to make a copy for him.

Ray Genet with the baby bonnet

About that time, a solitary figure was walking along the street either walking toward or from the Tee Pee (Talkeetna Motel/Lounge). I did not recognize him but Ray did. It was Milton Lichtenwalner. Ray usually used only the person's last name but in this case he called out for Milton to join us. Now when Milton approached us there was a small wire fence between him and us. (Now that I recall the event, it is probable that he was walking from the Tee Pee). Anyway, Milton approached the fence and with a graceful leap was sailing over the fence. The only problem was that Milton's lower foot was about 23 inches off the ground and the top of the fence was about 24 inches off the ground. When foot met fence, the foot stopped. The rest of Milton's body continued forward quickly being pivoted about the stationary foot. The whole scene appeared to be in slow motion with the first thing to contact the earth being Milton's face. Thankfully there had been a lot of recent rain and the grass was high, thick, and soft. Milton landed with a soft thud. Ray called out, "Mind the fence Milton". Ray and I both jumped up and rushed to his aid. We rolled him over and he had a smile on his face and was unhurt. We helped him up and Ray asked him to join us and share our brandy. Milton looked at the almost empty bottle and asked " Share what?" I don't remember if he didn't like the brandy, didn't want the brandy, or just ignored the brandy since there was so little left. We sat there for a while and didn't move even when a very light rain, almost a mist, started. After the brandy was finished and we had solved the major problems of the world, including some pressing issues in Talkeetna, we all got up and went our separate ways.

Ray and I remained friends until that sad day in November a couple of years later when I heard he had died on Mt. Everest. He had asked me to lead the last climb on Mt. McKinley that season a few months before he left for Everest. I had to tell him because of my work I could not get the time off for the climb. He therefore had to lead that last climb which meant he led three McKinley climbs that season. He said he had the flu or a cold that fall before he left for Everest and I'm sure he did not have his normal strength for that climb.

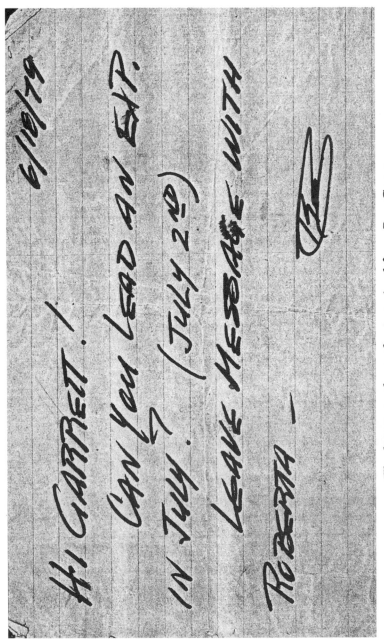

The last note the author received from Ray Genet

THE ROADHOUSE CURFEW

I need to explain the legend of the dreaded "Roadhouse Curfew." Carroll and Verna Close as the owners of the Roadhouse liked to run a tight ship and were very strict about the time of the evening meal that was served family style. Carroll was also very strict about when the guests were expected to be back at the Roadhouse in the evenings. He explained that some of the guests had to get up early in the mornings to go to work and that he and Verna also had to get up early and he would not allow any guests to be out drinking and come in late and disturb everyone. ("If they want to drink late at the Fairview Inn, let them sleep at the Fairview Inn!") Everyone was expected to be back by 10 p.m. when Carroll would lock the doors.

During my tenure at the Roadhouse, I never saw Carroll refuse to let a guest back in after 10 p.m. but I did see several severely reprimanded at the door. A typical scene might go like this: Someone would be knocking on the door for several minutes that could easily and obviously be heard but Carroll would ignore. Finally he would go to the door and yell without opening the door, "We're full tonight, try the Fairview or Tee-Pee (the Talkeetna Motel)." Voice from outside, "I'm staying here, I'm in room 4, Smith, I checked in this afternoon." Carroll would ignore the knocking for a while but then finally go back and open the door. He might say, "I said we're full tonight, you'll have to go somewhere else." The guest would then explain to Carroll who he was and that he was sorry he was late and give some excuse which Carroll would laugh at. I remember one inebriated guest trying to explain to Carroll how he got lost returning from the Fairview Inn, which is about 125 yards away on the same street. I have heard from reputable sources that Carroll has on more than one occasion refused to go to the door after hours and the late guests did have to get another room elsewhere.

While I was working at the Roadhouse for Carroll and Verna, I had to follow the same rules and be back by 10 p.m. However, on one November Saturday night there was a dance at the Tee-Pee and everyone was having a good time. Some of the locals knew I was staying at the Roadhouse and they enjoyed reminding me of the approaching curfew time. Some said that Carroll wouldn't lock me out since I worked for him but I knew and most of the other locals knew that he would lock me out. So at 9:50 p.m. I left the dance amid much heckling and more than a little reluctance since I was having quite a good time, particularly with a young woman from Anchorage. When I got to the Roadhouse (a very short walk) Carroll announced he was just about to lock the doors. I told him I knew that and I had just come back to get my sleeping bag since I was going to stay out for a little longer. He asked why and I told him about the dance but not about the young woman from Anchorage. He said he would leave the door open for me for a little while if I wouldn't be much later. I told him thanks, but I might be late and he should go ahead and lock the doors. He looked around to make sure no one was watching and went to the back door with me. He told me never to tell anyone about this but he hid the key so I could let myself in later. I thanked him and told him I'd try not to be too late.

I went back to the dance and had a good time but kept my drinking to a sociable minimum — it's one thing to return to the Roadhouse late, but it's entirely different to return late and drunk! Anyway, I left the dance around 1:15 a.m. and walked back to the Roadhouse mentally rehearsing how I would get the key, unlock the door, and creep to my room with complete silence. I arrived at the back door and stood quietly for a couple of minutes and I heard no sounds from within. I got the key, unlocked the door and went to my room and made absolutely no sound. The highest technology sound surveillance equipment would have not detected my entry or movement. Before I went to sleep I thought how nice it was of Carroll to let me stay out after curfew. I was also very happy I was able to get inside and to my room without disturbing them.

The next morning at breakfast he commented quietly to me where Verna couldn't hear, "1:30? I guess you had a good time!" I asked how did he know as I did not make a sound when I returned. He didn't answer but just gave me that Carroll Close smile and walked away.

Jim Gleason's painting of a Roadhouse winter

Jim Gleason painting of the Roadhouse

COLD SHOWER

One winter afternoon I had been doing something for Carroll and had become quite sweaty and dirty. I asked him if the wood stove that heated the water for the showers had been started. As there was not a guest at the Roadhouse that evening, Carroll had not started a fire. I asked him if I could start the fire because I was very dirty and wanted to take a shower before dinner. He said O.K. but to make it a small one since there were no guests.

I started the fire and as it took about thirty or forty minutes for the water to be hot, I went outside to do something. Just before I returned, a guest arrived and Carroll told him he would have time to take a shower before dinner. The guest took his shower and turned off the water just as it was starting to cool. He evidently was in the shower for quite some time to use almost all of the hot water!

I returned to the Roadhouse and checked on the fire. It was almost out so I thought there was plenty of hot water for me. I undressed and got into the shower. The water was only luke-warm but I thought the real hot water was on the way so I got completely soaped up and was preparing to rinse off under the wonderful hot water I was expecting any second. To my surprise and shock, the water turned very cold very fast! The water supply was from a well and the water temperature was about 40° F. (Alaska well water is cold!) I immediately jumped to the side of the shower stall thinking I had hit the temperature controller or perhaps this was just a brief flash of cold water for some unknown reason. The water only got colder. I tried to think what had happened but I finally realized that for some reason there was no more hot water. I found myself completely covered with soap with very cold water coming out of the shower. I knew I had to rinse off so I planned how to do it as quickly as possible. I reached out and placed my towel on the bath room door so I could get to it easily for my planned very rapid drying operation. Having my plan fully thought out it was now time for implementation. I moved back under the stream of cold water and tried to move around very fast so that each part of my body was only exposed to the very cold water for as short a time as possible. I can not truly relate to the reader how cold that water was. After I had most of the soap off, I pulled back the shower curtain and jumped out away from the cold water, planning to reach back in and turn the water off. As I jumped out, I grabbed for my towel hanging on the door. At this point, implementation of the plan began to deteriorate. Evidently some water had splashed out on the floor and when I jumped out I slipped just as I was grabbing my towel. As I fell to the floor with a loud crash, I pulled the towel from the door and also pulled the door open. As I came to rest, wet and naked on the floor with the towel in one hand covering nothing, I looked up and saw Carroll who had just happened to be walking by the bathroom door.

Carroll opened his mouth to say whatever was appropriate for such a situation. Then, he evidently thought there was really not an appropriate comment that could be made, so he simply smiled and reached over and closed the door.

VERNA'S BINGO CROWD

One fall day it was raining quite hard and it was one of those Alaska rains that looked like it would last for days. Verna was going to her Bingo party over at the VFW or at the Catholic Church, I can't remember. She asked me if I would like to go but I said I didn't think I could because Carroll might need some help. She saw him and asked if he would let me go with her since he really wasn't going to need me with all of the rain. Carroll said O.K. and winked at me and said have a good time. He knew I wasn't a big Bingo fan but I would have to go since Verna had asked.

So off we went. There were about fifteen other women there, I was the only man. The person in charge asked how many cards I wanted so I said one. Everyone laughed at that and commented that most played twelve but some of the older women could only play eight without holding up the game. Having been ridiculed even before the game started, I sheepishly agreed to play four cards. I sat to the left of Verna so, as she said, she could help me if I needed it.

The game started but the women were still all talking to each other and only quickly glanced at their cards. Now I must point out that I have completed quite a few math courses and consider myself good with numbers, but let me tell you I was in the room with a bunch of sharks and was out of their league in finding the called numbers on my cards. A number would be called and I would start looking for it on my four cards but before I had looked at all of my cards, Verna would either point to the number on one of my cards or say, "You don't have it." She would do this after checking her twelve cards first. This woman could check twelve cards and then check my four cards before I could check my four cards! I was astounded. I was amazed. I was mortified and embarrassed. I have never felt like such a dud in my life. The crowning blow came later when a number was called and Verna immediately cleaned off the tokens from her cards. The lady next to her asked what she was doing and she said, "Ron has a Bingo on his third card." I hadn't even had time to look at my third card yet!

Somehow I survived the afternoon and returned to the Roadhouse a beaten man. I think all of the women had a great time laughing at me toiling over my four cards and I'm sure my play was the subject of laughter at the Bingo games for quite a few years. Later that night I told Carroll about my ordeal and he just laughed. He said he understood and that if those women were as good at poker as they were at Bingo, they would own the town!

Verna Close on Main Street with Kate Sheldon and "Boots."

THE ROADHOUSE AS A SOCIAL CENTER

During the 1960s and early 1970s, the Roadhouse was often host to social activities such as dances, game nights, engagement parties, holiday dinners, and other events, particularly during the winters. (The famous Roadhouse poker games will be discussed in another section.) Although during the period of my stay only a few of such activities occurred, Verna often would mention past parties and gatherings. I have included a few photographs from these earlier times so readers will be able to see some of the activities as well as a few of the participants.

Roadhouse Living Room, 1962; Orvil Ingelhorn, Vera Robeson, Dotty Wohlgemuth, Mary Jean Toughluck.

Engagement party, 1961; Verna Close, Suzy and Jim Kellard, Nick Rubino.

Christmas Dinner, early 1960s; Verna and Carroll Close, Norm and June Schebel, Milt Lichtenwalner, Harry Robb.

Saturday Night Dance, 1960s; Bill and Nancy Powell (standing), Eleanor Rubino and Loyd Wohlgemuth (dancing), Norm Schebel.

Saturday Night Dance, 1960s; Gloria Brittian, Dotty Wohlgemuth, Nancy Powell.

87

Saturday Night Dance, 1960s; Nick Rubino, Verna Close, Loyd Wohlgemuth, Donny McKinsey.

Colonel Johnson, 1969.

KEY TO THE CITY

In the fall of 1976, when Verna and Carroll had been operating the Talkeetna Roadhouse for 25 years, some of the locals decided it was a good time to recognize them for this record. A small party was held at the Roadhouse with just a few close friends attending to celebrate with the Closes. Jim Kellard handcrafted a wood placard to commemorate the event. The accompanying photograph shows this placard, which was presented to the Closes at the party. A late decision was made to add the "Key To The City" as part of the celebration.

Celebrating 25 years at the Roadhouse

ROADHOUSE POKER GAMES

The Roadhouse poker games were legendary. However, since I only participated in one game, I can not relay much first hand information. Since I do not pass on second hand information in these stories, the factual reporting of the Roadhouse poker games will be limited. I will not mention any names in this matter because, although a lot of time has passed, many of the participants are still living in Talkeetna. As an extra concern, some are married, and some even have the same wives as they did during that time. Most will understand the need for privacy in this somewhat delicate matter. I have included a rare photograph from a Roadhouse poker game. The reader will notice that the privacy of the players has been assured except, of course, I left Carroll Close's image untouched.

Most games were held at the Roadhouse but rarely some were held elsewhere in Talkeetna because of reasons on which I will not comment. Without exception, the game was conducted on a table covered with an army blanket. Carroll would have his silver dollars, which he kept in a National Bank of Alaska bag, and the players would exchange some of their folding money for Carroll's silver dollars. The games were played using these silver dollars and folding money. After the game the players would return the silver dollars to Carroll for exchange since the silver dollars were used only for the game and Carroll always retained them.

The one game I did attend left a lasting impression. I had played a little poker in my time but my experience was mostly in fun poker, cheap games which were actually more of a social event than gambling. The first thing that attracted my attention was there were no coins in sight. My thought was how were we going to handle 25 and 50 cent bets. I quickly learned that would not be a problem. I believe on the first hand I reached in my pocket and took out a quarter and placed it on the table for a bet. Everyone looked at me and I believe Carroll looked at the quarter and asked what it was for. When I told the group it was my bet everyone laughed and someone suggested to Carroll that he was not paying his help enough. Carroll politely suggested that coins were not used in the games.

I stayed for a while, I hope long enough to have not embarrassed myself, but I could see right away that most of the players had more money that I did, or at least were willing to risk more money than I would. Additionally, and perhaps of even more importance, all of the players seemed to be better at poker than I was. I quickly assembled this information and came to a very rapid conclusion that this was not the place for me! After a while I excused myself with the best excuse I could think of at the time. I believe I was asked a couple of other times if I wanted to attend a poker game but I always had some pre thought out reason which prevented my attendance. These were probably just courtesy invitations anyway. The Roadhouse poker games were a part of that time and were keenly anticipated and enjoyed by a good number of the Talkeetna men.

Roadhouse Poker Game

MICROWAVE IN THE ROADHOUSE

Carroll and Verna Close sold the Roadhouse in 1978. Later that summer, during one of the town festivals, I ran into them on Main Street. We talked for a while about how they were doing in Palmer and how the new Roadhouse owners were doing. Verna started talking with some other women so I drew Carroll off a few feet and said I had to tell him something. I looked warily up and down the street and around us to give him the impression that what I was about to tell him was very important and private and I did not want anyone else to hear. He got close and was eager to hear what I was going to say. "Carroll," I said, "They've installed a microwave oven in the Roadhouse." His response was almost a jerk backwards. If I had told him they were performing abortions in the first bathroom I don't thing he would have been more shocked. He shook his head and muttered, "You don't have a microwave in a roadhouse," and slowly walked back to where Verna was standing.

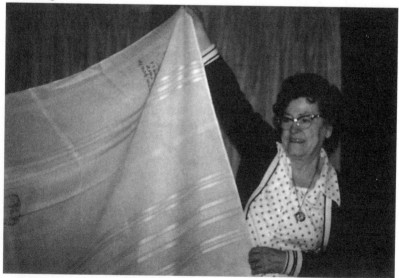

Verna with the tablecloth presented to her by the Talkeetna Homemakers Club at the going away party given when she and Carroll sold the Roadhouse and retired

93

ROADHOUSE RECIPES

ROADHOUSE SALAD DRESSING

Carroll and Verna Close always served salad with the evening meal. It was described as a mixed salad but it appeared to me as a salad of lettuce mixed with minute traces of other things. One night I took a close look at the "other things" in an attempt to identify them. I was tempted to use a magnifying glass to aid in my investigation but was afraid that Carroll or Verna might question me and I had no real confidence that I could respond with an answer which would satisfy them or the other guests who might be present. Careful observation led me to believe the "other things" were carrot parts, radish parts, and tomato stains. I can not truthfully report that I saw a tomato or a piece of a tomato but I can report that I believe a piece of a tomato had been in the vicinity of the salad. Perhaps one had been shaken up with the salad and then removed to be used again. It is possible I may be exaggerating the scarcity of tomato but I do not remember a Roadhouse salad that was overwhelmed with tomatoes.

Anyway, the "mixed" salad was quite delicious, I believe, because of the Roadhouse salad dressing. Of course no salad dressing was on the table, the dressing was put on the salad before it was taken to the table in a large bowl. I asked Verna several times about the salad dressing and she finally told me how it was made.

5 ounces Heinz apple cider distilled vinegar
9 ounces Crisco cooking oil (Wesson oil is O.K. but not as
            good)
1 cup sugar
mix and pour over salad

ROADHOUSE BREAD PUDDING

The famous Roadhouse bread pudding was one of my favorites. It was not served frequently because the standard Roadhouse dessert was vanilla ice cream. I would always ask Verna when she was going to make the bread pudding and she would reply, "Pretty soon." I don't think Carroll liked Verna to make the bread pudding because it did take some extra time and I believe Carroll wanted to just serve vanilla ice cream. One day I wanted the bread pudding so much that I told Verna I would help her make it. She laughed and said she was going to make some that day and she would appreciate some help. Carroll was off somewhere so I quickly moved to start the process hoping we would be so far along that Carroll wouldn't stop it. He did return after we had started and I will admit he did show some alarm when he saw me next to Verna covered with some of the ingredients for the bread pudding. When he learned what we were making he commented that I should help seeing how much of the bread pudding I ate the last time it was served. Verna responded that she didn't think I ate that much. Carroll replied that the last time bread pudding was served I ate more than the two mountain climbers that were there that night. I weakly replied that I ate more bread pudding that night because I didn't think the rich bread pudding would be good for the mountain climbers who had just returned from Mt. McKinley. Carroll smiled broadly and walked away.

first bowl: coat bowl with butter
>> *break up dried bread (or dry in oven before) into bowl

*put milk and butter on stove, heat just before boiling

second bowl: beat 3 eggs in a bowl
>> add 2 coffee cups of sugar
>> add about one egg size of cinnamon
>> add about 1 tablespoon of vanilla

put ¾ pound dark raisins into bowl with bread
pour milk into second bowl and then mix well and pour mix-
        ture over bread
push bread in and make sure all pieces are wet
sprinkle cinnamon on top of mixture
set bowl in a pan of water
cook 1½ hours in a preheated 375° F. oven.

* The observant reader will notice that quantities are not given for the bread, milk and butter. I would think the experienced cook will be able to take this basic recipe and do the right thing. I briefly considered estimating these quantities but I was afraid I might make serious errors in the estimates so I decided to come clean and admit I forgot to write down these quantities. The author sincerely apologizes for this oversight. (To have the original document created over twenty years ago is something approaching a miracle.)

THE AUTHOR'S FAMOUS BLACK RUSSIAN CAKE

At some time in the cloudy past I obtained a recipe for a Black Russian cake. I must hasten to add I did not originate this recipe but probably ripped it out of a magazine in some waiting room. I had made the cake a couple of times to rave reviews. I think the rave reviews were mostly a result of the cake's alcohol content because it seemed the most ardent compliments came from those who ate the most. Anyway, shortly after the bread pudding incident, I announced to Verna and Carroll that I would like to make my famous Black Russian cake in the Roadhouse. Carroll did not seem too excited at this suggestion, probably because he was still recovering from seeing me in the kitchen helping with the bread pudding. Verna was excited and wanted to know the recipe. I told her it was a secret but if she liked it I would tell her. She said O.K. and said we would make the cake that day. I went to my room and brought out all of the ingredients. (I had planned to make the cake at a friend's house before my culinary challenged mind thought of making it at the Roadhouse.) The cake was made and consumed on the spot by Carroll, Verna, Ray Genet, the author, and two other Roadhouse regulars. Verna liked it and said she had never tasted anything quite like it. Carroll said it was too sweet and could not be served with children around because of the alcohol content. Ray Genet loved it and said I should make another one next spring to take on the mountain. The other Roadhouse regulars loved it and suggested Carroll include it on the menu. Carroll scoffed at this suggestion.

The famous Black Russian cake was never again made or served at the Roadhouse although it was, in good humor, requested on several occasions.

18½ ounces deep chocolate cake mix
4 ounces chocolate pudding mix
4 eggs
¾ cup strong coffee
½ cup oil
¾ cup Kahlua and Creme de Cacao
mix and place in a bundt cake pan
bake 45 minutes at 350° F.

Frosting   1 cup powdered sugar
                1 tablespoon strong coffee
                2 tablespoons Kahlua
                2 tablespoons Creme de Cacao
                pour over cake and punch with toothpick to
                allow frosting to seep into cake

BOILED RAISIN CAKE

1 cup raisins
2 cups water

Boil together until 1 cup water is left

Cool

Add: 1/2 cup shortening
1 cup sugar
1 beaten egg
2 cups sifted flour
1 tsp. cinnamon
1 tsp. allspice
1/2 tsp. salt
1 tsp. soda
1/2 cup walnuts

Bake in loaf pan at 350 for 1 to 1 1/4 hours or until well done

RHUBARB CAKE

Mix 2 cups diced rhubarb and 1/2 cup sugar

Let sit

Cream 1/2 cup shortening and 1 1/2 cups granulated sugar

Add 2 lightly beaten eggs

Mix in flour sifter:
2 cups flour
1 tsp. soda

Dash of salt
1 tsp. cinnamon

Add to egg mixture alternately with 1 cup sour milk and
1 tsp. vanilla

Add to rhubarb and sugar mixture

Bake in layer or loaf pan at 350 for about 45 minutes

Serve plain or with ice cream or whipped cream

SHARON'S FAMOUS SWEET POTATO CASSEROLE

This recipe was never made at the Roadhouse. Being from the South, the author tried on more than one occasion to convince Carroll of the wonderful taste and food value of the sweet potato. This was in vain in that Carroll only served white potatoes. This recipe was given to me by my cousin from Huntsville, Alabama and the only reason I am including it is because it is SO GOOD!

3 cups cooked, mashed sweet potatoes (I think yams are
                   used most of the time)
1 cup sugar
2 eggs
1 teaspoon vanilla
½ cup milk
½ cup butter
cream together and put into 2 quart casserole dish

Topping
1 cup firmly packed brown sugar
⅓ cup flour
1 cup chopped pecans
⅓ cup butter
mix topping until crumbly and sprinkle on top

bake 30 minutes at 350° F.

ORDER FORM

LIFE AT THE
TALKEETNA ROADHOUSE

NAME: _____

ADDRESS: _____

CITY: _____ STATE: _____ ZIP: _____

TELEPHONE: (_____) _____

Price: $9.95

Sales Tax: Please add 8.1% for books shipped to Washington state addresses ($0.80)

Shipping: Book rate: $2.00 for the first book and 75 cents for each additional book. (Surface shipping may take three to four weeks)
Priority mail: $3.85 (or current postal rate) for one or two books.

Payment: Check or money order payable to:

ALIEN PUBLISHING
P.O. Box 10617
Spokane, WA 99209-0617

ORDER FORM

LIFE AT THE
TALKEETNA ROADHOUSE

NAME: _____

ADDRESS: _____

CITY: _____ STATE: _____ ZIP: _____

TELEPHONE: (_____) _____

Price: $9.95

Sales Tax: Please add 8.1% for books shipped to Washington state addresses ($0.80)

Shipping: Book rate: $2.00 for the first book and 75 cents for each additional book. (Surface shipping may take three to four weeks)
Priority mail: $3.85 (or current postal rate) for one or two books.

Payment: Check or money order payable to:

ALIEN PUBLISHING
P.O. Box 10617
Spokane, WA 99209-0617